JACK LONDON:

THE FORGOTTEN CHAMPION

BY

ARCHIE POTTS

BEWICK PRESS

First published in Great Britain by
Bewick Press
132 Claremont Road
Whitley Bay
Tyne and Wear
NE26 3TX

ISBN 1 898880 07 7

Typeset by Sumner Type, London SE22

Printed and bound in Great Britain by
TUPS
30 Lime Street
Newcastle upon Tyne
NE1 1P

ACKNOWLEDGEMENTS

I am grateful to Jack Clansey, Brian London and Bob Smith for recounting some memories of Jack London, and would like to thank the staffs of the British Newspaper Library at Colindale, Hartlepool Central Library, Newcastle Central Library and Sunderland Central Library for allowing me to consult their files of newspapers and periodicals. Most of the photographs in the book are from the late Owen Hughes' collection now in my possession, and John Jarrett was good enough to let me borrow others from his stock of boxing memorabilia. In addition, I should like to thank the editors of the *Hartlepool Mail* and *Sunderland Echo* for giving me permission to reproduce some of their press photographs. Vic Hardwicke kindly provided Jack London's boxing record and Dave Temple gave invaluable assistance on design and layout. Finally, I owe a huge debt to Mabel Challinor for the many hours she spent preparing the manuscript for publication.

ARCHIE POTTS,
Gosforth,
Newcastle upon Tyne.
October 1997.

CONTENTS

INTRODUCTION

Ask the question : 'Who was Jack London?' and most people would answer 'an American writer, the author of *The Call of the Wild* and *The Iron Heel.*' Some boxing buffs might remember a boxer of that name who won the British and Empire heavyweight titles back in 1944. But the truth is that Jack London, the former heavyweight champion, is largely forgotten. He won the title during the war years when the coverage of sport was at a minimum, and even during the late 1930s, when he was in his prime, he was denied a crack at the title and received purses far below his worth. One boxing writer has referred to him as British boxing's Cinderella man. The fact that Jack London was the father of Brian London, the British and Empire heavyweight champion 1958-59, is perhaps better known than the details of Jack London's career. Jack London was certainly no world beater: but, then, very few British heavyweight titleholders have been in that class. He was, however, a worthy British champion and was unfortunate not to have fought for the title when he was five years younger.

Part of Jack's trouble was that he lacked 'glamour'. He was prematurely bald and always looked older than his years, and he never had the physique of an Adonis. Nor was he in any sense a ring artist. His style was often described as 'crude' or 'lumbering', although his opponents found him sharp enough in the ring and Tommy Loughran, a former world champion who fought London, described him as 'the best boxer I have met in England'. London had a good left hook and a sharp left jab, but he lacked a crisp knockout punch although he could pound an opponent to defeat with his powerful right swings to the head or body. Jack London also lacked consistency : he would string together a good sequence of wins against top-notch opponents only to turn in a lacklustre performance when he was expected to do well. He was never popular with sports writers who rarely gave him any credit for his victories, and he chose to operate from his home base in West Hartlepool, far from London where title fights were often brokered. His career would have been different if he had enjoyed the patronage of a London promoter. Not that quiet-spoken Jack was ever heard to complain: he was tough and resilient and kept plodding on until he finally won the British and Empire titles in 1944. This is his story and readers unfamiliar with his record will be surprised to learn that he fought many of the top heavyweights of his time and proved more than a match for quite a few of them.

1

YOUNG JACK

Jack London was born John George Harper at Green Street, Stranton, West Hartlepool on 21 June 1913, the son of Tom and Eva Harper. Jack's father was a sea-going marine engineer by trade but he was working as a fitter in a local engineering works when his son was born. West Hartlepool was then at the height of its prosperity. It was a Victorian town built alongside the older town of Hartlepool as a port for the shipment of coal from the Durham coalfield and it had grown rapidly into a centre for steelmaking and shipbuilding. In 1913 the town had a population of 65,000 and boasted three theatres, two skating rinks, and half a dozen cinemas. Seven years later, however, the town's docks, steelworks and shipyards were hit by the post-war recession and young John grew up in the shadow of the heavy unemployment of the 1920s.

When John, or Jack as he was better known, left school at the age of 14 there were not many job vacancies in the town and it was a case of picking up what employment he could. At the age of 16 Jack went to sea, working on a tramp steamer carrying pit-props from Russia to West Hartlepool. Jack did not like the sea and when he arrived back in home port he switched his job to unloading the pit-props from the timber boats. This was hard work, for the pit-props – some of them weighing a cwt. – had to be unloaded by hand. The job was well paid by the standards of the time – £2 a week was good pay for a teenager in the 1920s – and the heavy manual labour helped to develop his arms and body.

In the evenings he used to go for eight mile runs with a local milkman nicknamed 'Chukker'. Chukker got Jack a lighter job working as a milk roundsman, but Jack had a lifelong love of animals and he could not resist opening an occasional bottle of milk to give a stray dog or cat a drink. Once his employer discovered what was happening the cost of the milk was deducted from his pay and after a couple of months in the job Jack was sacked. Jack had learned to drive a milk float and he then moved on to big trucks, earning a living as a lorry driver.

The future Jack London lived a few streets away from the Redworth Street boxing stadium converted from a disused joinery works. Boxing was well established in the town and its theatres, skating rinks and sports grounds had been used as venues for boxing before the conversion of the Redworth Street factory into a boxing stadium. Indeed, bare-knuckle fights had taken place on Seaton sands in the 19th century and boxing matches under Marquess of Queensberry rules are known to have been staged at the Church Street Athenaeum Club in the 1890s. By the turn of the century Ikey Carter had opened his Tin Circus boxing booth opposite the Sun Hotel in Lynn Street, followed by Bob Morton's conversion of stables on the corner of Burbank Street into a boxing booth which became known as the Bloodtub.

Why boxing should have had such a big following in West Hartlepool is difficult to explain, yet popular it undoubtedly was and the town has produced some good fighters. In Edwardian times Jasper Carter, a ring artist, learned his trade at the Tin Circus and went on to defeat the Irish and South African champions. Heavyweight boxers are never very thick on the ground in any age, yet West Hartlepool produced Jack Strongbow and Dick Bartlett, two useful heavyweights who were both contemporaries of Jack London. In the 1930s there were boxers such as Gunner Ainsley, Fred Baxter, George Bunter, Al Capone, Billy Clayton, and Billy Nicholson. Teddy Gardner won the British, Empire and European flyweight titles in 1952, and Jackie Horseman was the Northern Area featherweight champion 1951-1955. In more recent times

John Feeney was British bantamweight champion 1981-1985, his brother George held the British lightweight title 1982-1985, and Michael Cichoki won the Northern Area light middleweight title in 1993. George Bowes, who fought Johnny Caldwell for the British bantamweight title in 1964, now runs a gym in Hartlepool and the Borough Hall is still used for boxing, where matches are promoted by Gus Robinson.

The young John Harper was a fit and hefty lad and it is hardly surprising that he was drawn to boxing, donning the gloves as an amateur at the age of twelve, and as a teenager he sometimes fought bare-fist bouts with local pit lads on the sands at Seaton Carew with a ten shilling side-stake for the winner. It was one way of earning a bit of extra pocket money. Jack boxed and trained in local gyms with a young man seven years older than himself called John Stephenson. Both were determined to enter the professional ranks, and both fancied the ring name 'Jack London'. Why had the name 'Jack London' taken their fancy? Jack London was a popular novelist and they both liked his books but London was also a boxing correspondent and they had read some of his fight reports in American boxing magazines. Obviously there could not be two Jack Londons in the British ring so they tossed a coin to see who would claim the name and Jack Harper won. The loser John Stephenson chose the ring name 'Jack Strongbow' and he fought under this name against Battling Manners at Darlington on 12 June1931, and a month later his friend, the newly named Jack London, met Barney Stockton at the Redworth Street Stadium in West Hartlepool on 10 July 1931. Barney Stockton was a local favourite and Jack London was drafted in as a last minute substitute against him. London weighed in at over 11 stones and was the heavier man of the two, and he made his weight advantage count against his more experienced opponent, knocking Barney Stockton out in the first round. Jack was paid 12s 6d for his first fight in the professional ranks.

A week later London was in action again when he beat Battling Manners in the first round on a disqualification. To win a fight on a disqualification is always unsatisfactory and it left Hartlepool fight fans wondering: how good is London? Two days later London knocked out Phil Henry in the fifth round at Stockton, and 11 days after this he won a 10 round points victory over Jack Wharton at Middlesbrough. Jack Wharton was a stockily built bulldog of a fighter from Sunderland. He was three years older than London with six years of ring experience behind him and he was never an easy man to beat. A fortnight later London travelled to Newcastle where he defeated Jim Williams on points over 10 rounds. London had won his first five professional fights and already there was a division of opinion about his potential. Some believed he had the makings of a future champion and others that he was a tough lad with a powerful punch but likely to be no more than this.

Jack London travelled to Royton for his next fight, where he was outpointed over 12 rounds by Rochdale's Eddie Strawer. No one can say that London was being given easy fights: his sixth bout was a 12 rounder against a hard-hitting opponent with a big following in Lancashire. London returned to his home town for his next fight where he knocked out Corporal Ingledew in the seventh round.

London lost his next four fights against Tommy Moore, Jack Smith, Tom Powell and Willie Duncan by points decisions then knocked out Jim Williams in the second round of a return contest. He returned to New St James Hall to face Sunderland's Frank Bagley. London charged in on Bagley from the opening bell, throwing left hooks and right swings, but Bagley successfully countered London's rushes.and used his left jab to good effect. The referee awarded Bagley the verdict on points. London had three more fights before the end of the year: knocking out Tom Powell in the sixth round, then being outpointed by Chris Rock and Jack Smith.

Looking back at the end of 1931 on his first six months in the professional ranks, London could mark up eight wins against eight defeats. He had been pitched in against some hard, experienced men and had come through his baptism of fire with credit. He had proved that he could take a punch as well as throw one and his ringcraft was improving with every fight. He was still only 18 years of age, six foot in height with a big frame and already a light heavyweight. It was clear that he would mature into a fully-fledged heavyweight. Many saw him, even at this early stage, as a future British heavyweight champion.

Another big change in Jack's life in 1931 was that he married Agnes Rossborland and they set up home in a small terraced house in Brenda Road, only a few streets away from the Redworth Street boxing stadium where London had many of his early fights. As a newly married man Jack needed to fight as often as he could to bring in the money, and he was soon earning higher rates as he made his way up the bill. He was paid 25 shillings for fighting Phil Henry in his third professional fight and £3 – 10s for tackling Jack Wharton at Middlesbrough, when he topped the bill for the first time in his boxing career. It was another three years before he was to earn £100 for a single bout. Walter Hazeltine, who worked as a clerk in a local paperworks, ran the Redworth Street Stadium and he had the reputation of being a generous promoter. He gave the boxers as much as he could afford and never screwed them for every penny as did some promoters. Nevertheless his stadium only held a thousand spectators and he had to keep entrance charges down during the depression years, therefore the purses he could offer were low : a fiver was good pay for someone topping the bill at small stadiums such as Redworth Street.

In 1932 Jack London had 15 contests and he recorded 10 wins, three losses and two draws. By now London had built up a strong local following and 12 of these contests took place in his home town, one in neighbouring Stockton, and one in Newcastle upon Tyne, and for the remaining contest Jack made his first trip to London.

London started the year by fighting a draw with Frank Bagley in a return match and scoring a win over Joe Morrison. In February he fought Jack Clansey from Sunderland and lost on points over 10 rounds. London was criticised by some for his lacklustre performance against Clansey, but this takes credit away from Clansey who fought a clever fight, keeping clear of London's hooks and swings and darting in with his left jab. Clansey made London look slow and clumsy: he was a smart fighter who outfoxed big Jack on this occasion. There was talk of arranging a return match between the two men, but for whatever reason it never took place. In later years Jack Clansey always regarded his victory over London as one of the high points of his boxing career.

For his fourth fight of 1932, London met Dick Bartlett from the same town and the stadium was packed by local fight fans eager to see these two up-and-coming fighters in action. Bartlett had turned professional in 1930 and after some early knockout victories had been dubbed the 'Hartlepool White Hope'. Although he never lived up to this billing in subsequent bouts Dick Bartlett was a crowd pleaser who liked a good scrap. Jack London was prepared to trade punch for punch and he was awarded the decision over Bartlett on points. In an attempt to reverse an earlier defeat, London was matched for a third time with Frank Bagley and the outcome was another draw over ten rounds.

London then stopped Gunner Ainsley in nine rounds. Jim Ainsley was born in Wingate, a colliery village seven miles outside Hartlepool, and he had served in the Royal Artillery where he had won the brigade's heavyweight championship when stationed at Woolwich. He had turned professional in 1922 and although a '12 stoner' he often fought above his weight, taking on light heavyweights and heavyweights in order to keep busy. London did well to stop him in nine rounds and Ainsley was impressed with his young opponent. Ainsley trained at a gym in Todd's Square in Hartlepool's Headland district and he encouraged Jack London to train with him. The former gunner taught young Jack many tricks of the trade and he took a close interest in London's boxing career.

London had now matured into a heavyweight and he continued on a winning streak, knocking out Coporal Dorry in one round, Dick Bartlett in five rounds, forcing Tom Powell's retirement in three, and defeating Paul McGuire on points.

He then faced Charlie McDonald in a catchweight contest at the Redworth Street Stadium. For this fight London weighed 13st. 3lb. and McDonald 11st. 7lb. The bronze-skinned boxer from Sunderland was giving away nearly two stones in weight to London, but he was vastly more experienced and an accomplished master of the 'sweet science'. It was full house at the stadium as the fans flocked to see this match. London went all out to score a knockout, throwing punches at McDonald from the opening bell, but McDonald slipped London's leads and piled up the points with his counter-punching. The referee had no hesitation in naming McDonald the winner on points over 12 rounds. London was undeterred by this defeat and in his next fight he took only three rounds to dispose of Bill Brennan, and then went on to defeat the 6ft 4in giant, Guardsman Gater, on points over 12 rounds.

2

INTO THE TOP TEN

On 23 October 1932 Jack London travelled down to London for his first fight in the capital city. Up to this date all his fights had taken place in Northern England with the exception of a fight against Willie Duncan in Edinburgh. Twenty-six of his bouts had taken place in the North East of England plus one trip to Lancashire and another to Yorkshire. London promoters, however, were reading reports of a promising young heavyweight called Jack London and they wanted to see him in action. London made his metropolitan debut at the Blackfriars Ring where he was matched against Jack O'Malley, who was billed as the heavyweight champion of Australia. London, therefore, was not being handed an easy fight and the match was intended to put O'Malley in the shop window as much as London. The London promoters were interested in measuring the abilities of both men for possible use on future bills. A first-class heavyweight was worth his weight in gold to them.

London started extremely well: he caught O'Malley with a right swing to the jaw in the first round and forced the Australian to take a short count. O'Malley was far from beaten, however, and he fought back with vigour. London was happy to mix it with him and it was an exciting bout until the seventh round when London was forced to retire with a damaged right hand.

London was back in action the following month when he started a sequence of eight fights without defeat which included seven wins and one bout declared no contest. On 2 December 1932 he met his local rival, Jack Strongbow. Strongbow was an old friend and former sparring partner of London's, but there was no old pals' act between the two men when they met in the ring. The fight was promoted by Walter Hazeltine at the Borough Hall, Hartlepool, and was refereed by Fred Charlton. Strongbow gave one of the best performances of his boxing career. He did all the forcing and piled up the points with his left jab. However London dropped him with a right to the chin in the ninth round but Strongbow was up in an instant and forced London back on the ropes with a flurry of punches. Then, at the end of the round with victory almost assured Strongbow had to announce his retirement with a damaged right hand.

Dick Bartlett and Jack London were rematched for a third meeting at West Hartlepool on 6 January 1932. Bartlett boxed defensively for the first three rounds and held London at bay, but after this Jack began to land his punches and he dropped Bartlett for a count of eight in the fifth round. In the sixth round a towel came fluttering into the ring from Bartlett's corner leaving Jack London the winner.

Ten days later London defeated Charlie McDonald on points over 12 rounds and one commentator remarked on how much London had improved since the pair had met six months before. McDonald boxed with his usual skill and coolness, but London had the edge on him this time.

London reversed another defeat in his next fight when he met Rochdale's Eddie Strawer. Strawer was still a middleweight and he came in at short notice as a substitute for the Stoke heavyweight, Bert Ikin, who was nursing a cut eye. Strawer was giving away two stones in weight to London and he boxed defensively in the first round, but in the second round he caught London with a peach of a left hook which dropped the big man for a short count. London got up and went for Strawer with every punch he had, stalking his man around the ring for the remaining eight rounds, but failing to land a knockout blow. London was awarded the decision on points and Strawer was cheered for his plucky performance.

Bert Ikin, a promising young heavyweight managed by Len Johnson, made his delayed appearance at West Hartlepool on 10 February 1932. The Stoke boxer was taller than London and he had a good straight left which won him the first three rounds. In the fourth round he suffered a cut eye and London began to get on top. He dropped Ikin for counts of eight in the fourth and eighth rounds and emerged a clear points winner. Ikin's game display had pleased the crowd and he was given a loud cheer when he left the ring.

London then finished off Jack Morris in six rounds but his next fight was a stinker. He faced Les Saunders from Rotherham and after three dull rounds the referee, Fred Charlton, sent the men back to their corners and declared the fight 'no contest'. Anxious to make up for the poor performance in his previous fight Jack London forced the pace from the opening bell when he met Battling Sullivan at West Hartlepool on 12 April 1933. Sullivan suffered a cut eye in the fourth round and his seconds threw in the towel in the following round.

London's winning streak was halted by Gipsy Daniels at Merthyr in Wales. Daniels real name was Billy and he was a Welshman. Early in his career he had travelled to the USA to gain experience in American rings. His American manager believed that he needed more 'colour' if he was to succeed in the States, so he made Daniels wear a bandana and ear rings and he sold him to the American press as the champion of the gipsies. The name stuck and for the rest of his life Billy was known as Gipsy Daniels. In fact, Daniels was a very fine boxer who did not need gimmicks. He won the British light heavyweight title in 1927 and in the following year he knocked out Max Schmeling in one round. In 1933, when he met London, he was rated number five among British heavyweights. London was holding his own against Daniels until he had to retire in round six with a damaged right hand.

Three weeks later London met the highly-rated Canadian fighter, Al Conquest, at the Brunswick Stadium, Leeds. The two hammered it out over 12 rounds and the decision was awarded to London. At Norton on 18 May 1933 Jack London knocked out Bobby Shields of Glasgow in the second round, and a week later London travelled to Wales where he defeated Tony Arpino on points over 15 rounds. Four days later he earned a draw with George Slack, a future Northern Area champion, and then defeated Battling Sullivan in a rematch.

In the mid 1930s North East England had several top class fighters in the lower divisions. Billy Charlton, Mickey Maguire, Douglas Parker, Benny Sharkey and Tommy Watson could hold their own against the best in the country and any of their names on a boxing bill was guaranteed to draw the crowds. There were far fewer top boxers in the higher divisions. In the early 30s the region's biggest draw was undoubtedly Jack Casey from Sunderland. 'Cast iron' Casey, as he was known because of his toughness, had fought Len Harvey for the British middleweight title in December 1932. In 1933 he was weighing in around 12 stone and taking on light heavyweights as well as middleweights in order to keep busy. The emergence of Jack London opened up the prospect of matching these two men from neighbouring towns.

The fight was eventually arranged to take place in the open-air at the Engineers' Club Grounds, West Hartlepool, on Monday 12 June 1933.

The match was billed:

> *The fight of a lifetime!*
> *Stupendous attraction!*
> *The question has got to be settled:*
> *Who is the hardest hitter in the North?*

And to emphasise local rivalries the undercard was made up entirely of Sunderland versus Hartlepool boxers. The ground capacity was 3,000. The promoters expected a full house and were not disappointed. Jack London had good local support and special trains were laid on from Sunderland to West Hartlepool to carry hundreds of Casey fans travelling to the fight. On the evening of the contest the stadium was lashed by torrential rain and spectators were soaked to the skin as they watched the preliminary bouts. Jack London was just 20 years of age, although he had packed 44 fights into his two and a half years of professional boxing and was in good form when he faced Casey. At the weigh-in on the afternoon of the

BOXING! **ENGINEERS'** CLUB GROUNDS. **BOXING!**
(Opposite Town Hall. Capacity 3,000.) Referee: T. H. CRAGGS.
(Licensed under the B.B. Board of Control.)
MONDAY, JUNE 12.—Doors Open 6-30 p.m. Commence, 7-30 p.m.
THE FIGHT OF A LIFETIME! Stupendous Attraction! 15 3-min. Rd. Contest.

JACK CASEY v. JACK LONDON
(Sunderland Assassin.)   (West Hartlepool.)
The Question has got to be settled—"Who is the Hardest Hitter in the North"?
Two 6-min. Rd. Contests.—TOMMY BEST (Sunderland) v. K.O. SHIPLEY (West)
JACK HUGHES (Sunderland) v. PRIVATE BATTLES (West)
Extra Special 10-Rd. Contest.—ROY MILLS (S'land) v. GEO. BUNTER (H'Pool)
PRICES (including Tax): 1/-, 2/6, 3/6. Ladies 1/- to all parts.—Seats can be
Booked at Central Hotel, also Engineers' Club.

BOXING ENGINEERS' CLUB GROUNDS, WEST H-POOL **BOXING**
MONDAY, JULY 17.   Doors Open. 6.30. Commence, 7.30 p.m.
Extra Special Super Attraction at Enormous Expense, 12 3-Min. Round Contest.

GIPSY DANIELS   versus   JACK LONDON

(Wales). Beaten Phil Scott. Reg. Meen. Max Schmeling. Peirre Charles (draw), Jack Strongbow. Seaman Rowles. Boxed Wal Neusel to a close decision.

(West Hartlepool). Record: Jack Slack, Chas. McDonald, Paul McGuire, Willie Unwin, Jack O'Malley, Eddie Strawyer, Bert Ikin, Al Conquest. Bobby Shields, Dick Bartlett, Jack Strongbow. Jim Ainsley, etc., etc.

DANIELS ARRIVED LAST NIGHT AT 6.30.   There will be a public weigh-in at 2 p.m.

LIVERPOOL STADIUM (Adjoining EXCHANGE STATION)
THE FINEST BOXING HALL IN GREAT BRITAIN
TO-MORROW, THURSDAY, AUG. 31st. at 7.45   LIVERPOOL STADIUM LTD. PRESENT
TWO 12 ROUND CONTESTS   (Under the Direction of Johnny Best)

LEN JOHNSON v. JACK LONDON
(MANCHESTER).   (WEST HARTLEPOOL).
The Famous Coloured Boxer.   The Coming Heavy-weight Sensation.
TONY BUTCHER (LIVERPOOL) v. PETER NOLAN (WALSALL)
Recently Boxed a Tarrilling Contest, Butcher Winning.
TWO 10 ROUND AND OTHER CONTESTS

Tickets Obtained from STADIUM (Telephone) Bank 4/27)
JACK SHARP Whitechapel   RUSHWORTH & DREAPER, Islington   PIER HEAD HOTEL CHEETE
    LADIES ADMITTED
Special Summer Prices.   RESERVED, All Bookable Seats
(Including Tax) 7/6 Ringside 1st 3 Rows and 5/9 3/6 Circle 2/6 Outer Circle | 1/3 unreserved

---

*Advertisements 1933: top two from 'Northern Daily Mail'
and bottom advertisement from 'Boxing' magazine.*

contest he had a two stone weight advantage over the Sunderland man.

Casey was a battle-hardened veteran of seven years in the professional ranks. He had fought the best in the game, including Marcel Thil, Jock McAvoy and Len Harvey. Casey was as tough as they come with a jaw that had been likened to concrete and a skull as hard as a cannonball. He was immensely strong and could deliver a knockout punch with either hand.

When the opening bell rang, Casey came out of his corner in his customary crouch with his head stuck out and hands held low. He went straight into the attack, looking for an early knockout. But London fighting in traditional English upright style, was not overwhelmed and he used his powerful left jab to hold Casey off. Having survived Casey's opening onslaught London began to get on top and he dropped Casey in the fourth round, although the cast-iron man was back on his feet before the referee started to count. Thereafter it was London all the way as he pounded Casey almost at will, dropping him for a second time in the tenth round. At this point some people in the crowd began to wonder if London might turn out to be the first man to knock out Jack Casey. Certainly London was well ahead on points and apparently heading for a comfortable victory. Then in the interval between rounds 10 and 11, London announced his retirement and held up his right hand to indicate an injury.

It was a sensational end to the fight and London was criticised by some of his supporters for not fighting on. He was far ahead on points and Casey looked well beaten. Could London not have nursed his right hand for the last five rounds and won a points victory? It always looks easier to those outside the ring than it does to those who are fighting inside it, and London decided to retire. He was suffering pain from his injured hand and Casey was a dangerous opponent who never gave up until the final bell. Five rounds was a long time to survive and London felt that he needed two good hands if he was to continue to face up to Casey.

In spite of his defeat by Casey, when the next edition of *Boxing* magazine came out in July 1933 Jack London was rated among the

top ten British heavyweights. The compiler, Neville Buckley, wrote:
'the only name added to the prevailing crop of heavyweights is that
of Jack London, the young West Hartlepool boxer, whose recent
performances have made it plain that he must not be excluded on
any account.'

The full listing was:

Champion: Jack Petersen, Cardiff.
Contender: Jack Doyle, Dublin.
      1.   Jack Pettifer, Brighton.
      2.   Charlie Smith, Deptford.
      3.   Harry Crossley, Doncaster.
      4.   Eddie Steele, South Norwood.
      5.   Gipsy Daniels, Newport.
      6.   Seaman Rowles, Chatham.
      7.   Jack London, West Hartlepool.
      8.   Reggie Meen, Mexborough.

Jack London was to be included in the top ten ratings of Britain's
heavyweights for the rest of his boxing career.

3

THE MID-THIRTIES

Jack London was now recognised by Britain's premier boxing magazine as one of the country's leading heavyweights and he began to be matched against top-class boxers. Over the next few years he entered the ring against other highly-rated British boxers, and against boxers from other parts of the British Empire who had come to the United Kingdom hoping to find fame and fortune. He also fought some top European and American boxers.

After his defeat by Jack Casey, an examination of London's right hand had shown it to be badly bruised and not broken as feared. It responded quickly to treatment and a month later Jack London was back in action against the Dutch heavyweight Con Van Lowen. London was then rematched with Gipsy Daniels and lost narrowly on points after a hard-fought battle. In a third meeting of the two men London managed a draw. The Daniels-London bouts were fascinating contests between a wily old-timer and a rising youngster. London's next opponent, Len Johnson, was another crafty boxer of vast experience and he outpointed London over 15 rounds. This proved to be the last victory of Len Johnson's long boxing career, after two more fights he retired from the ring. Meeting master boxers such as Daniels and Johnson was an invaluable part of London's education in ringcraft. London followed up with a victory over Johnny Rice.

On 6 November 1933 London had his first taste of big-time

boxing when he met Ben Foord the fighting Springbok in the top-of the-bill contest at Crystal Palace. The old Crystal Palace on Sydenham Hill was a Victorian structure of glass and iron, and was one of London's most famous landmarks. It had been refurbished in the 1920s and began to be used for sporting events. Boxing promotions began there in 1933 and continued until 1935 when the building was destroyed in a spectacular fire. Jack London appeared on seven boxing bills at the old Palace and he turned in some good performances in front of big crowds.

London's opponent, Ben Foord, was a big, strong, tough South African fighter. He had competed in swimming, running and rugby before becoming a professional boxer in his native country. He had arrived in Britain in 1933 in search of the Empire title, and after two years residence in the UK he would be eligible to compete for the British title. In fact, he won the British and Empire titles in August 1936 when he defeated Jack Petersen over three rounds and lost the titles to Tommy Farr seven months later. He had already beaten the highly-rated Charlie Smith when he was matched with Jack London as part of his build-up campaign.

London was a provincial heavyweight having his second fight in the capital city. He was something of an unknown quantity to many spectators in the hall and if Foord was expecting an easy fight he did not get it. London proved an awkward opponent and although Foord deserved his narrow points victory over 10 rounds *Boxing* magazine's reporter at the fight believed that if the contest had been over 12 rounds London would have won. London always had the capacity to grind an opponent down over the course of a bout.

London returned to the Crystal Palace a month later when he was matched with Seaman Rowles. London floored Rowles in the first round but was unable to follow through and the tar struggled gamely to survive the 12 rounds. At the final bell London was awarded the decision on points.

A week later Jack London faced his stiffest test to date. On 11 December 1933 he met Larry Gains at New St James' Hall. Gains, a black Canadian boxer, was the British Empire champion. In 1933 he was in his prime and a formidable opponent. It was a great

CRYSTAL PALACE

MONDAY NEXT, Nov. 6, at 8 p.m.

HULLS' BOXING PROMOTIONS Present Another BIG SHOW at Popular Prices.

Heavy-weight Contest—Ten (3 min.) Rounds

Ben Foord v. Jack London
(South Africa)   (West Hartlepool)

Other Ten (3 min.) Rounds Contests

Dave Finn   v.   Tommy Hyams

George Daly   v.   Jim Wheeler

AND OTHER BOXING

SEATS (Including Tax and Admission to the Palace)

3/6, 6/- 10/6 Numbered & Reserved   **1/10** Unreserved

BOOK NOW: Crystal Palace (Phone: Sydenham 7333)
Keith Prowse & Co., Ltd., & Alfred Hays, Ltd.

CRYSTAL PALACE

MONDAY NEXT, Dec. 4th, at 8 p.m.

Heavy-weight Contest—Twelve (3 min.) Rounds

SEAMAN HARRY   JACK

ROWLES v. LONDON
(Royal Navy)   (West Hartlepool)

Heavy-weight Competition

Giants from all parts of Great Britain will compete

FOR £200 in Prize Money AND A BELT

SEATS (Including Tax and Admission to the Palace)

3/6, 6/-, 10/6, Numbered & Reserved   **1/10** Unreserved

BOOK NOW: Crystal Palace (Phone: Sydenham 7333)
Hulls' Boxing Promotions, 22, Chudleigh Rd., S.E.4
(Phone: Lee Green 3540)
Keith Prowse & Co., Ltd., & Alfred Hays, Ltd.

Posters for fights at the Crystal Palace 1933.

opportunity for London to make his mark: a good performance would have boosted his reputation and he was paid £100, the first time he had earned three figures for a bout. Unfortunately London found himself overmatched. He started well, carrying the fight to Gains in the first round and catching the champion with a couple of good punches. In the second round, however, Gains cut loose and knocked out the younger man with a body punch just above the belt. Some people in the crowd shouted, 'Foul!' and 'Low blow!' but the referee ignored their protests and London later confirmed that it had been a perfectly legitimate blow. It was the first time London had been knocked out in his boxing career.

One of Jack London's greatest strengths was his resilience. When knocked down he would pick himself up from the canvas and carry on, and this is what he did after his defeat at Gains' hands. However 1934 was a patchy year for him and it started with disappointment. At Crystal Palace on 15 January, London was matched with Charlie Smith and the understanding was that the winner would meet Jack Petersen, the ex-British heavyweight champion, at Cardiff. Unfortunately for London he lost a narrow points decision to Charlie Smith and Smith got the fight with Petersen. In the event the match did not enhance Smith's reputation: he was knocked out by Petersen within twelve seconds of the opening bell. How London would have fared against Petersen can only be subject of speculation but he could hardly have done worse than Charlie Smith.

London went on to score wins over George Slack, Frank Borrington, Jack Strongbow, Johnny Rice, Alex Bell and Italo Colonello but lost decisions to Bert Melzow and Charlie Belanger, and suffered knockouts at the hands of Pierre Charles and Charlie Belanger (in a return match); and he earned a creditable draw against Jack Pettifer.

Pierre Charles was the Belgian heavyweight champion and London agreed to fight him in Ostend. Jack travelled down to Harwich by train and then by boat to Ostend. The sea crossing was very rough and London, never a good sailor, was violently sea-sick. He had not fully recovered from the effects of the voyage when he entered the ring against Charles, and at the first good punch Charles landed London went down and stayed down. After his retirement from the ring London admitted that this was the only time in his entire boxing career that he did not attempt to beat the count. He had not exactly taken a dive, for he felt groggy at the start of the fight, but he made no effort to get off the canvas and carry on with the bout. The Belgian promoter was no fool and he realised what London had done and he tried to withheld payment, but after much haggling London was paid his £110 purse money. After this incident London always insisted on travelling abroad by air.

In the following year he did much better when he lost only two fights: he dropped a decision to Alex Bell on a disqualification and was defeated by Ben Foord in a rematch. He had wins over Frank Borrington, Jack Pettifer, George Slack, Jack Casey, Helmuth Hartkopp and Charlie Smith; and he entered a heavyweight competition at Wembley where he defeated Jack Strongbow, Ginger Hauxwell and Johnny Rice – the final was 12 months later when London beat Pat Marrinan on a disqualification. London rounded off 1935 with a win over Eddie Steele.

The year 1936 started well for London but went sour towards the end. He began with a six rounds points victory over Eddie Houghton, fighting on the undercard of the Jack Petersen versus Len Harvey British and Empire heavyweight title match at Wembley Stadium; and followed up with victories over Roy Lazer, Frank Borrington and Maurice Strickland. Then on 16 March he faced Tommy Loughran over ten rounds at Bristol.

Loughran had held the world light heavyweight title 1927-29. He then moved up into the-heavyweight ranks and fought Primo Carnera for the world heavyweight title in March 1934, when he was defeated on points by the Italian giant. Loughran was a polished boxer, what the Americans call a 'fancy Dan', and he made Jack London look crude. London, however, gave him a hard fight: in the closing rounds he realised that Loughran was well ahead on points and he went all out to score a knockout. Loughran was awarded the decision on points but London had performed well before an appreciative crowd. When Tommy Loughran returned to America he described Jack London as 'the most dangerous fighter in Europe' – high praise indeed from such a quarter.

Three months later Jack London was in the ring against another top-notch American – Obie Walker. Walker was a black fighter from the USA, and he had earned the reputation of being a knockout specialist with a mean streak. He had been brought over to Europe by promoter Jeff Dickson, who had difficulty in finding the 'black terror' suitable opponents. Jack London accepted the offer of a match and he tamed the American over 10 rounds to win on points.

In October London travelled to Berlin to take part in a heavyweight boxing tournament promoted by Walter Rothenburg at the Deutschland Hall, a big sports hall built in the 1920s and refurbished for use in the 1936 Berlin Olympics. Rothenburg's promotion was the first time the hall had been used for professional boxing. Jack London was one of three British boxers who took part in the tournament. Alex Bell from Scotland lost narrowly on points to Werner Selle and Frank Hough the 'fighting hussar' gained a narrow points victory over Leonard Marohn. Before an audience of 16,000 Jack London faced Hans Schonrath of Germany. Schonrath bored in on London in the early rounds and in the fourth round he caught him with a punch below the belt. It was a clear foul and justified disqualification, but London insisted that he be allowed to carry on and the referee gave him a minute to recover before waving the two men on again. London's sportsmanship earned him the cheers of the crowd and he went on to score a 10 round points victory over the German. After the tournament all the winners, including London, were presented with a victory medal, and on London's return he was awarded a certificate of merit by *Boxing* magazine for his performance against Schonrath.

But how quickly the tides of fortune can change. Twelve days after the Schonrath fight, Jack London was rematched with Larry Gains at Earls Court. At their previous meeting Gains had knocked out London in the first round, on this occasion both men showed excessive caution and after eight dull rounds the referee stopped the fight and declared it 'no contest'. For some reason, many sports journalists blamed London for the fiasco, and Gains's reputation emerged unscathed. Yet it takes two men to bring about a no contest verdict and Gains was as much to blame for the lack of action in the fight as was London.

London returned to the capital in November to meet Pat Marrinan in the final of the heavyweight competition held over from the previous year which he won by a disqualification in the sixth round.

London ended the year by issuing an open challenge to Tommy Farr, the leading contender for the British title. This was a forlorn hope, for the Welshman stood on the brink of fame and fortune and he was unlikely to want to step into the ring with Jack London at this particular point in time. Tommy Farr had endured years of poor purses and lack of recognition and this was about to change. In March 1937 he won the British and Empire heavyweight titles, followed this up with victories over Max Baer and Walter Neusel, and in August he fought Joe Louis for the heavyweight championship of the world.

CERTIFICATE OF MERIT

"THE WATCHER'S" award for the best performance of the week goes to JACK LONDON, of West Hartlepool, for defeating Hans Schonrath, of Germany, in Berlin.

JACK
LONDON

21 year old Heavy-weight Sensation and Crystal Palace favourite,

will fight Peterson for Pa's top hat, Doyle for his Mayfair flat, and Gains for fun.

Has fought Pierre Charles, Gains, Belanger, Pettifer, Foord, Borrington, Charlie Smith, Rowles, Len Johnson.

Apply:

68, BRENDA RD., WEST HARTLEPOOL

JACK LONDON
OF WEST HARTLEPOOL
CHALLENGES
TOMMY FARR
HEAVY-WEIGHT CHAMPION OF WALES
to a contest over twelve or fifteen rounds for
£250 A SIDE
Money will be deposited with " Boxing " or the B.B.B. of C. as soon as Tommy Farr says ' Yes.'
All coms.
J. LONDON, 68, BRENDA ROAD, WEST HARTLEPOOL

Jack London challenges Jack Petersen, Jack Doyle and Larry Gains in 'Boxing' 22 August 1934 (above) and Tommy Farr in the same magazine on 2 December 1936.

4

PRIME TIME

London was probably at his fighting best over the period 1937 to 1939, but two things eluded him. First, he never made big money during the boxing boom of the 1930s. Although he often topped the bill at premier promotions, he was rarely paid more than £100 for any of his fights. One hundred pounds was a worthwhile sum in the 1930s but it was a poor purse compared to those earned by some other top heavyweights such as Jack Doyle. Doyle, dubbed the 'Irish nightingale' because of his talent as a singer, was a major box office attraction and could pick up anything from £2,000 to £3,000 for a single fight. The contrast between the handsome, debonaire Jack Doyle and the homely Jack London could not have been greater. 'Glamour', to use the contemporary term, was a popular commodity in the 1930s and it applied to boxing as much as it did to other entertainments. London was married with two young sons to support and between bouts he worked as a lorry driver in his home town : there were no winter cruises or sunny Californian beaches for him.

Secondly, he never got a crack at a British or Empire title. In spite of being rated among the best, the Boxing Board of Control failed to include London among those chosen to fight for a title or even to give him the chance of fighting in an eliminating bout against other contenders. No doubt the Board of Control had its reasons and, as always, luck and circumstances played their part in denying Jack London the opportunity of fighting for a title when he was at his peak.

Jack London was even denied a shot at the Northern Area heavyweight championship. The title was held by Doncaster's George Slack, who won it in 1932 and had successfully defended it on five occasions. On 25 January 1937 Jack London was matched against Bob Carvill of Bridlington in an eliminating bout for the Northern title. The fight was staged at West Hartlepool and Jack London gained a points victory over 15 rounds. Two months later London met George Bennett of Manchester at New St. James's Hall in a final eliminator and he knocked out Bennett in the second round. This win established London as the leading contender and John Paget, the Newcastle promoter, obtained approval from the Boxing Board of Control for George Slack to defend his title against Jack London. The purse money on offer was £86 split 60 per cent for the champion and 40 per cent for the challenger. This offer proved to be unacceptable to Slack who said that after expenses and commission had been deducted he would be fighting for almost nothing. As a result Slack was stripped of his title by the Board of Control and the fight with London never took place. Con O'Kelly and Harry Lister were matched for the vacant title in the following year.

Jack London started 1937 with a points win over Bob Carvill and then lost on points to Dutch champion, Harry Staal. He knocked out Pancho Villar of Spain in two rounds at Bristol and did the same to George Bennett at Newcastle. He was then matched with Buddy Baer at Swansea.

Buddy was the younger brother of former world heavyweight champion, Max, and he had ambitions to follow in his brother's footsteps and become world champion. Buddy stood 6ft 6ins in his socks and weighed 17 stone. He had a knockout punch and had disposed of Jack Doyle in one round at Madison Square Gardens two years before. Buddy Baer had come to Europe to notch up a few more wins in support of his campaign for a crack at the world title, however there were few fighters keen to climb into the ring with him. Eventually, promoter Syd Hulls offered the match to Jack

London with a purse of £400 – by far the biggest of his career up to that time- and London agreed to meet the American giant.

Baer caught London with some heavy punches in the early rounds and forced him to take several counts, but Jack got up and fought back. As the fight progressed he began to wear Baer down and in the last two rounds London was well on top. Jack, however, had left it too late and Baer was awarded the decision on points.

A couple of months later London returned to Swansea where he knocked out the Welsh heavyweight, Jim Wilde, in the third round. In Jack London's last fight of 1937 he knocked out Manuel Abrew, a black heavyweight from Edinburgh, in the sixth round.

Jack London's first fight in the new year was a return match with the German fighter, Hans Schonrath, resulting in another points victory for London, and in a rematch with Harry Staal he reversed a previous defeat by beating the Dutchman on points over 10 rounds. In June Jack London's father died and Jack was contracted to meet Al Delaney on the twenty-third of the month at New Cross. Perhaps Jack would have been wiser to have withdrawn from this fight but he chose to meet his commitment. Not surprisingly, he was not at his best, for his father – Tom Harper – was usually in his corner and this added to his sense of loss. London fouled Delaney with a careless punch in the fourth round and was disqualified. Once recovered from his bereavement Jack London went on to defeat Harry Lister, Joe Zeman, Charlie Bundy, Al Delaney (in a return contest), Alf Luxton and George Cook.

One of the most significant events in the British boxing world in 1938 was Tommy Farr's relinquishment of his British title because of his commitments in the USA. Would Jack London, who was very much in form, get his chance? In spite of several articles and letters of support in *Boxing* magazine, London was not involved, not even in an eliminating bout. Len Harvey and Eddie Phillips were matched by the Boxing Board of Control to fight for the vacant title, and Harvey duly became British heavyweight champion on 1 December 1938 after Phillips had been disqualified in the fourth round for a low blow. Harvey went on to pick up the Empire heavyweight title three months later by defeating the holder Larry Gains.

Jack London challenged Harvey for a crack at the title, but Harvey was hoping for a championship defence against Tommy Farr which he, rightly, saw would be a big money spinner. Tommy Farr returned from the USA in February 1939 and after defeating Red Burman in a return match in April said he was interested in winning back the British and Empire heavyweight titles held by Len Harvey. In May, Farr stopped Larry Gains in five rounds and afterwards issued a title challenge to Harvey. Len Harvey was amenable to meeting Farr with the championship at stake but his demand for a purse of £7,000 meant that Farr's end of the gate would be very low if the match was to be financially viable, and promoter Syd Hulls, who was interested in staging the fight, pulled out of negotiations.

The London promoter, A.J.Elvin, then stepped in with a proposal to stage a Tommy Farr − Jack London match in the open-air at St. James's Park, the home of Newcastle United. The last time boxing had been staged on the famous ground had been in 1916 when Bombardier Billy Wells, the British champion, had fought Sergeant Dick Smith in a charity contest in aid of the Red Cross. The bout had attracted 12,000 spectators and there is no doubt that a Farr − London fight would have drawn the crowds. Both Farr and London, not to mention the promoter, could have expected a good pay-day and the winner of the bout would have established himself as the leading contender for Harvey's titles. Preparations for the fight were well advanced, with Saturday 5 August 1939 being pencilled in as the date for the proposed bout, when the Freemen of Newcastle, from whom the ground was rented, announced that they would not give their approval for the stadium to be used for this purpose, and the deal fell through.

A new twist to the proposed Farr − London bout was then provided by the Welsh Boxing Board. The Swansea promoter, Bert James, had originally proposed to match Tommy Farr against the German heavyweight, Arno Koeblin, but the Welsh Boxing Board declined to recommend that the German be granted a work permit by the Ministry of Labour and instead the Board proposed that Jack London should be Farr's next opponent.

Jack London 1932.

Green Street, Hartlepool, in 1997. The terrace house where Jack London was born was demolished in the 1960s

The Borough Hall in Hartlepool where Jack London fought in the 1930s. The building is still used for boxing matches.

Seaman Rowles.

*Jack London in training for his
second fight with Ben Foord.*

Ben Foord.

Frank Borrington.

Obie Walker

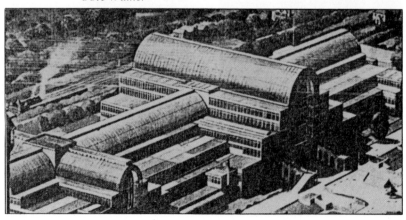

The Crystal Palace where Jack London fought several bouts before the glass-domed building was destroyed by fire in 1935.

The Deutschlandhalle, Berlin, where Jack London defeated Hans Schonrath on the 7 October 1936.

Jack London spars up to Buddy Baer, Swansea 24 May 1937.

L ONDON, whose real name is John George Harper, was little known in London when he fought Ben Foord, then beginning to make his name, and lost narrowly on points at the Crystal Palace four years ago.

Since that time London, who is 24 years old, has fought most of the leading heavyweights, and has won considerably more fights than he has lost. Even those he has not beaten have been given hard fights by London.

After Buddy Baer, the giant American, had beaten Jim Wilde at Harringay in four rounds he fought London at Swansea. Not only did Baer fail to knock out London, but the points decision for the American was most unpopular.

In his last fight London knocked out Jim Wilde in three rounds at Swansea last August.

London has beaten Pancho Villar, Charlie Smith, Roy Lazer, Hans Schonrath, Obie Walker and Maurice Strickland. He ran Tommy Loughran to a very close decision.

Extract from boxing programme for the Harringay Arena 29 November 1937. Jack London knocked out Manuel Abrew in the sixth round.

Jack London pounds Larry Gains to defeat at the Liverpool Stadium on 25 January 1941.

Jack London throws a right hand punch at Tommy Martin when they met at Earls Court on November 1939. Martin won on points.

Freddie Mills and Jack London square up to each other in their battle for the British and Empire heavyweight titles at Belle Vue, Manchester, on 15 September 1944.

Above: Sergeant J.G. Harper.

Left: A dip in the sea - Jack London in training for the Woodcock fight.

Jack London is welcomed home as the new champion.

Jack London with his wife and sons outside the Olympia Exhibition in London, shortly before he defended his titles against Bruce Woodcock.

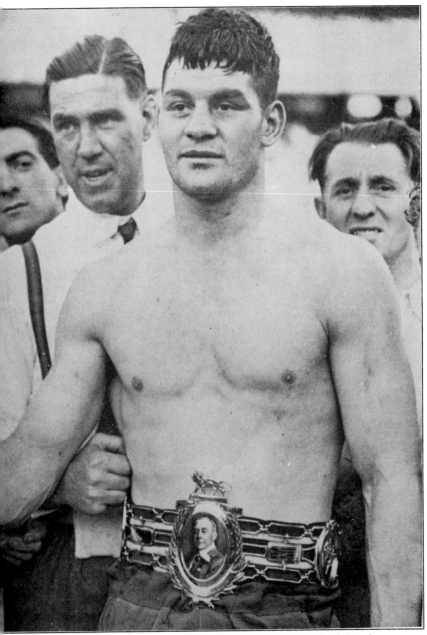

ce Woodcock sports the Lonsdale Belt after his victory over Jack London.

Jack London versus Bruce Woodcock at White Hart Lane on 17 July 1945

Jack London faces James Britt at the Engineers' Club grounds, West Hartlepool, on 5 May 1947

Jack Pye, who tried to persuade Jack London to take up wrestling.

Tony Baer, the Scottish wrestler who tangled with Jack London when they served together in the RAF.

Aaron Wilson ends Jack London's boxing career with a left hook to the head at Earls Court on 29 November 1949.

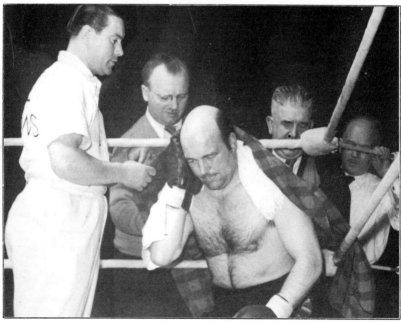

Jack London nurses his injured ear.

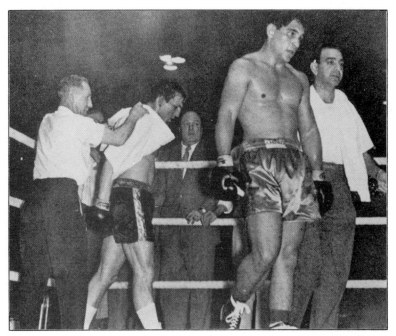

Jack London looks on as Willie Pastrano is given the decision over his son, Brian, at Harringay Arena on 25 February 1958.

Brian London spars with his father in preparation for his fight with Joe Erskine for the British and Empire heavyweight titles.

Jack London congratulates Brian on becoming the new champion.

The London family pose before Brian's 1959 world title fight against Floyd Patterson.

The Secretary of the Welsh Board explained:

London has made several appearances in South Wales and we felt after declining to recommend a permit for Koeblin that London should get a chance in an important contest. Our members realise that London is in the front rank of heavyweights and a capable opponent for Farr. Actually Farr wished us to approve of his opponent and we have selected London.

London was enjoying a holiday in Skegness, after his one round victory over the Belgian heavyweight Jean Verbeeran, when the Welsh Board made its announcement, and when informed said he would get into training for the bout as soon as he had finished his holiday. London was not given to boasting and he had the greatest respect for Tommy Farr yet he fancied his chances against the Welshman:

If Farr traded punches with me in the same manner that he did against Red Burman the fight would not go the distance. I'd gamble I can take everything that Farr can send over, but whether Farr could stand up to my punching is doubtful. I think I have the beating of him.

The Mayor of West Hartlepool said that he and several other local councillors would be travelling to Swansea to watch the bout, and the LNER announced that it would be putting on a special train to take London supporters to Swansea.

These arrangements, however, turned out to be premature. When Tommy Farr was approached by the press for his comments on the proposed match, he said that he had not yet been consulted about the terms on offer and he added 'I shall want the lion's share of the gate.'

When Jack London and John Joyce, a West Hartlepool bookmaker who handled Jack London's financial affairs, travelled down to London to finalise terms and sign the contract they believed that agreement with Farr would be a formality. They were wrong : Farr refused the terms on offer. Jack London had been offered a guaranteed payment of £159 plus 20 per cent of an estimated gate of £3,000 after deduction of tax. London, therefore, stood to pick up £750 for the fight and was happy with those terms. Farr would be paid around £2,000 and it was not enough to satisfy him. 'I have nothing against London', said Farr. 'But boxing is a business and I will not enter the ring unless I am satisfied that it is worth my while to do so.' He added: 'If a northern promoter can come up with an improved offer I should be happy to consider it.'

These events were taking place against a background of growing international tension. Throughout August, Hitler demanded that Danzig should be handed over to him and on 1 September 1939 he invaded Poland. Two days later Britain and France declared war on Germany. The proposed bout between Farr and London had been provisionally arranged to take place on 5 September at the St Helen's Rugby Ground in Swansea and even if the terms had been agreed and contracts signed it would have been cancelled following the outbreak of war. A Farr-London fight is one of the great might-have-beens of British boxing and Jack London always regretted that he was never given the opportunity of fighting the Welshman.

Jack London enlisted in the RAF, where after basic training at Padgate he completed a six week physical training instructors' (PTI) course at Uxbridge from which he emerged as Corporal J. G. Harper, wearing a PTI's badge above his two stripes. He was then posted to St Athan in South Wales. St Athan was at this time the largest RAF maintenance unit in the UK, a sprawling camp of hangars and workshops where aircraft were stored and repaired. Corporal Harper was on the staff of the station's sports section which contained a number of other prominent sportsmen who were serving as PTIs in the RAF. Midway through the war he was posted from St Athan to the RAF unit at Squires Gate on the southern outskirts of Blackpool. Squires Gate had an airfield from which Defiants and Hurricanes operated as part of North West England's air defences, and it was also home to a Coastal Command training unit. The war-time RAF station is now the site of Blackpool airport. London had been promoted to sergeant and was a senior member of staff in the sports section. He was demobilised from Squires Gate in 1945.

The impact of the war on the careers of sportsmen varied considerably. At one extreme some sportsmen were killed or wounded in action, others spent the war in POW camps, and there were many who were forced to curtail sporting activities for the duration of the war. Jack London was lucky. Like Freddie Mills he was a physical training instructor in the RAF. He had NCO's rank with its protection and privileges. His job was to keep RAF personnel in good physical shape and to do this he had to be fit himself. He was also expected to box exhibition bouts before audiences of airmen as part of the RAF's entertainment programme. He had access to RAF gyms for training and, as was also the case with Freddie Mills, he had commanding officers who were prepared to give him the time off to fight in the professional ring. Len Harvey also joined the RAF where he became a physical training instructor and was then commissioned. As an officer he was heavily involved in administration. He was unable to take time off to train or fight and, as he himself admitted, there was plenty to eat and drink in the officers' mess. As a result he grew flabby and ring-rusty. Both Jack London and Freddie Mills took advantage of their wartime opportunities and won titles, Len Harvey lost his.

Jack London fitted in two fights in the winter of 1939 during the period of the 'phoney war' when most things carried on as normal. On 27 November he met Tommy Martin at Earls Court. Martin was a classy boxer from Deptford who was debarred from fighting for a British title because of his colour. He had a very interesting life after he left boxing: he served in the US Marines, ran a gym in Hollywood, and went to an American university where he trained to be a physiotherapist. Martin defeated London on points over 10 rounds. Jack London was back in the capital a fortnight later when he stopped Tom Reddington in the seventh round.

There was little sporting activity in 1940 when Britain was facing invasion and struggling to survive, and London had only one bout when he stopped Al Robinson in the third round at Newcastle upon Tyne. Things picked up a bit in 1941 and London knocked out an ageing Larry Gains at Liverpool, and knocked him out for a second time in a rematch staged in Newcastle. He also outpointed Tom

Reddington in a rematch. On 1 August he outpointed Tommy Martin at Manchester in what was billed as an eliminator for the British Empire title, and boxing correspondents who witnessed the fight said that they had never seen Jack London in better form. Four months later Jack London met Freddie Mills at the Royal Albert Hall and after 10 dull rounds Mills was awarded the decision on points. London had now been promoted to the rank of sergeant but he was still able to fit in a few contests. Owing to the war the pool of active boxers was small and fighters found themselves being rematched against each other. In 1942 he, once again, knocked out Larry Gains, and took only two rounds to dispose of Jim Wilde. In 1943 he repeated his knockout victory over Jim Wilde, stopped Al Robinson in eight rounds and in March 1944 he outpointed George James.

5

CHAMPION

On 20 June 1942 at the Tottenham Hotspur football stadium in White Hart Lane, 22-year-old Freddie Mills belted Len Harvey out of the ring in the second round to win the British and Empire light heavyweight titles. The 34-year-old Harvey, one of Britain's most accomplished boxers, had been widely fancied to retain the titles but a young Freddie Mills had proved too strong for him. Harvey, however, was still the British and Empire heavyweight champion but six months later he relinquished both titles and announced his retirement from the ring.

Freddie Mills, as the conqueror of Harvey, was obviously in line for a crack at the vacant heavyweight titles. Other names in contention were Jack London, Al Robinson, and Tom Reddington, although Jack London's record put him well ahead of the others. The Boxing Board decided that Freddie Mills should meet Jack London for the vacant titles and the fight was arranged to take place at London's Queensberry Club in September 1943. The choice of venue was criticised in the press because the Club could only accommodate 2,000 spectators and ticket prices would be beyond the pocket of the average boxing fan. However during his final work-out with sparring partner Tom Reddington, Jack London cracked a rib and the fight had to be postponed. The match was rearranged to take place at the Tottenham Hotspur football ground on 8 July 1944, was then switched to Leicester, and was finally staged at Belle Vue, Manchester, on 15 September 1944. The fight was promoted by the Northern Sportsmen's Charity Fund in aid of the RAF Benevolent Fund and selected children's hospitals.

This time there were no hitches and the contestants – both of them RAF physical training instructors – trained at their respective RAF stations. Jack London's sparring partners were : Jim Herlihy, an Irish heavyweight; Rex Arnold, Western Command heavyweight champion; Ted Husketh from Liverpool; and a Manchester heavyweight called Jimmy Saxton.

London had fought Freddie Mills in December 1941 when he had been beaten on points over 10 rounds, but he had learned something from that defeat. Big Jack knew that he would have to sharpen up if he hoped to beat the faster-moving light heavyweight champion, and in training sessions he concentrated on speeding up his movements in the ring. Although Mills had probably improved as a fighter since their last meeting nearly three years before, Jack London felt that he had the measure of fiery Freddie and was satisfied with his preparations for the championship bout.

In spite of the postponements the fight caught the public's fancy, and Freddie Mills was a 3-1 on favourite to win the titles. His sensational victory over Len Harvey had impressed many people and it was widely believed that` youth would be served once again when Mills stepped into the ring against the 31-year-old Jack London. Freddie Mills was immensely popular and since winning the light heavyweight titles he had become something of a celebrity. Boxing fans appreciated his toughness and aggressive style in the ring and the wider public were attracted by his ready grin, craggy features and mane of black hair. In contrast Jack London was bald and portly, looked older than his years, and although he had a good sense of humour he was a quiet-spoken man of few words. He was the underdog, as he had been for most of his boxing career, although the staging of the contest in Manchester meant that he enjoyed good support from the predominantly Northern crowd. Seven thousand people paid a total of £10,000 to watch the heavyweight bout and London was paid £1,550, by far the highest purse of his long ring career. A live commentary of the contest was

THE

QUEENSBERRY ALL-SERVICES CLUB

THE LONDON CASINO, OLD COMPTON STREET, W.1

President · THE MARQUESS OF QUEENSBERRY

OPEN TO NON-MEMBERS FOR THIS NIGHT ONLY

Wednesday, September 22nd at 6.30

Doors open at 5.30

THE MARQUESS OF QUEENSBERRY

presents for

THE HEAVYWEIGHT CHAMPIONSHIP OF GREAT BRITAIN and the BRITISH EMPIRE

And the Lord Lonsdale Heavyweight Championship Challenge Belt

A 15 THREE-MINUTE ROUNDS CONTEST

between

FREDDIE MILLS

Light Heavyweight Champion of the World

and

JACK LONDON

Officially appointed Contender for this Heavyweight Championship
And released by Courtesy of the Liverpool Stadium

AND FIVE OTHER OUTSTANDING CONTESTS
FEATURING STAR BOXERS

The Tournament which is under the Supervision and Match-making of
JOHN E. HARDING will be concluded not later than 9.30 p.m.

THE CHAMPIONSHIP CONTEST WILL TAKE PLACE AT 7.45

PRICES 25 gns. **10** gns **5** gns. **3** gns. **(all Reserved)**

Poster for the postponed fight between Freddie Mills and Jack London for the British and Empire heavyweight titles.

broadcast by the BBC and millions of people clustered round their radio sets to listen to the 'big fight'.

The two men entered the ring looking very fit – both these RAF sergeants had commanding officers who had allowed them time off to train for the fight. Although Mills was the favourite in the betting stakes, he was a light heavyweight, weighing in at 12st. 51/2lbs, tackling a fully-fledged heavyweight three stones heavier at 15st. 63/4 lbs with an added advantage in height and reach. Freddie Mills was as tough as they come in boxing, but Jack London was no cream puff and had proved over the years that he could take a good punch. Both men had come up the hard way. Mills, the former milk roundsman from Bournemouth, had worked in the boxing booths and fought on the small halls circuit; and Jack London, the lorry driver from West Hartlepool, had spent 13 years in the game.

Mills carried the fight to London over the first 10 rounds, using his left hook and his overarm right hand punch known to boxing fans as his 'Mills bomb'. London operated his powerful left jab like a piledriver as Mills came at him and swung over his right whenever he saw an opening. At the end of the 10 rounds Mills was ahead on points and London had sustained a small cut under his left eye. In the eleventh round, however, London switched his tactics: he began to direct more of his punches at Mills's body and Mills began to slow up. London piled on the pressure in round 14, switching his attack from head to body at will, and he completely dominated the fifteenth round, although Mills gamely stood his ground and took everything that was thrown at him.

When the referee, C.B.Thomas, raised Jack London's glove after the final bell there was loud applause from around the stadium, and Freddie Mills went across the ring to congratulate the new champion: 'Well done, Jack, you deserved to win if only because you have had to wait years for your first title chance.'

The fight report in *Boxing News* observed : 'by far the best heavyweight battle witnessed in this country for more years than one cares to reckon..........hard fought and thrilling........ as an exhibition of the sweet science it left so much to be desired – but then London and Mills have never pretended to to be ring artists.'

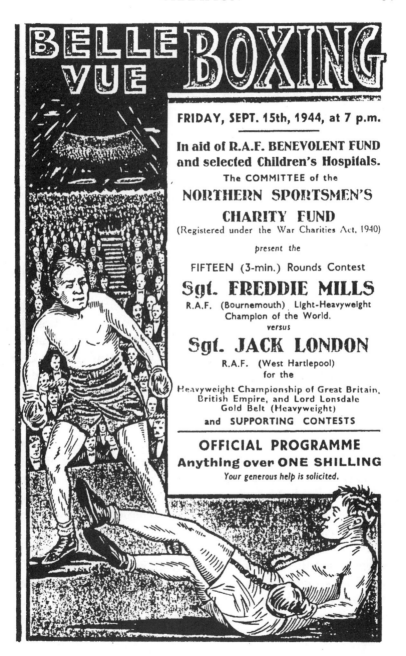

BELLE VUE BOXING

FRIDAY, SEPT. 15th, 1944, at 7 p.m.

In aid of R.A.F. BENEVOLENT FUND and selected Children's Hospitals.

The COMMITTEE of the

NORTHERN SPORTSMEN'S CHARITY FUND

(Registered under the War Charities Act, 1940)

present the

FIFTEEN (3-min.) Rounds Contest

Sgt. FREDDIE MILLS

R.A.F. (Bournemouth) Light-Heavyweight Champion of the World.

versus

Sgt. JACK LONDON

R.A.F. (West Hartlepool) for the

Heavyweight Championship of Great Britain, British Empire, and Lord Lonsdale Gold Belt (Heavyweight)

and SUPPORTING CONTESTS

OFFICIAL PROGRAMME
Anything over ONE SHILLING

Your generous help is solicited.

Henry Rose of the *Daily Express* had been one of the few sports journalists to forecast a London victory. He had written : 'If London can weather the early Mills blitz he will win on points', and he had been proved right. Jack London had paced himself very skilfully over the 15 rounds. He had worn Mills down over the first 10 rounds, while he retained reserves of strength and stamina for use over the last five rounds. London's tactics had gained him a narrow points victory over his opponent.

Those who had listened to the BBC radio commentary found that it was cut off at nine o'clock to make way for the news. The fight had reached the twelfth round with Freddie Mills ahead on points and apparently heading for victory. The sports commentator did not emphasise the way the fight was beginning to tilt in London's favour in the eleventh and twelfth rounds, and many listeners were surprised when it was announced at the end of the news that Jack London had won. On the basis of the radio commentary over the first 12 rounds they had assumed a Mills victory. When Jack London's victory was given out over the radio there was deep disappointment in Bournemouth and among the airmen at RAF Upavon but jubilation in West Hartlepool and at RAF Squires Gate.

When Jack London returned to his home town in September wearing a black homburg hat and dark overcoat, looking more like a prosperous businessman than a boxer, a huge crowd awaited him outside West Hartlepool station, and when he appeared they all sang, 'For he's a jolly good fellow.' He was, without doubt, West Hartlepool's most famous son and the town was proud of him. Two days later he was given a civic reception, and at the end of October he boxed an exhibition bout with his sparring partner , Rex Arnold, on a charity bill at the Borough Hall, Hartlepool, in aid of the Missions to Seamen building fund.

Jack London was now the British and Empire heavyweight champion and there was already speculation about a defence of his titles. The *Boxing News* wrote 'big Jack will be short of opposition in this country' and considered that Freddie Mills looked to be the only worthy contender. After their exciting championship encounter a London-Mills rematch would have pulled in the crowds and Jack

Solomons was eager to promote the contest in London. However the German V2 rocket campaign against the south of England forced Solomons to abandon his plans and shortly afterwards Freddie Mills was posted to India.

Jack Solomons' mind then turned to a promising young heavyweight called Bruce Woodcock, who had fought on the undercard of the Mills-London championship bill. Woodcock was a railway fitter from Doncaster. He had won the ABA light heavyweight title in 1939, turned professional in 1942 and had won the Northern Area light heavyweight championship in the same year. By 1945 he had 18 professional bouts behind him and had developed into a full-blown heavyweight, weighing in at 13 stone. His manager, Tom Hurst, was convinced that his young protege was ready for a British title fight and pressed hard for the match.

Jack Solomons, however, had to get Jack London's agreement and for the first time in his boxing career Jack was in a position to dictate his own terms. London's financial affairs were still being handled by John Joyce, and Solomons offered Joyce a purse of £1,500 for London to fight Woodcock. Joyce rejected this offer in pungent terms. After careful consideration Solomons telephoned Joyce with an improved offer of £3,000 and Joyce replied that £4,000 was the minimum he would consider. Jack Solomons broke out in a sweat and then took the plunge : 'OK, Mr Joyce, London gets £4,000", he gulped into the moistened mouthpiece.

The figure of £4,000 was a fair one : it was what Len Harvey had been paid for defending his light heavyweight titles three years before. Woodcock was paid £1,600, not a bad purse for someone of his experience who was getting an early crack at the title.

These figures show how unlucky Jack London was in regard to the date when he won the title. He won – and lost – the title just as British boxing was entering the big money era. Young fighters such as Woodcock and Mills were to reap the full financial rewards of being champions during the years of the post-war boxing boom. Jack London missed out on the big purses of the 1930s and the defence of his heavyweight titles in 1945 was the only really big purse of his boxing career. He earned almost as much in this single fight than he had made in all his previous fights put together.

Jack Solomons made a profit of £400 on the London-Woodcock fight. This was a poor return for the work and risk of putting on a major boxing promotion, but Jack Solomons considered it worthwhile because it established him as one of the country's leading promoters and he never looked back.

Jack London had a warm-up fight before he tackled Bruce Woodcock. On 15 June 1945 he met Scottish heavyweight, Ken Shaw, who was forced to retire with a damaged ear in the eighth round. This non-title bout was staged at the Hartlepool Victoria football ground and it allowed Jack to fight before a large crowd of his own supporters as the British and Empire heavyweight champion.

After this it was a month of solid training in preparation for the defence of his titles. Both Jack London and his opponent, Bruce Woodcock, were homespun men. Woodcock trained in a gym in the loft of a pub and did his roadwork in the country lanes around Doncaster. Jack London was granted leave from the RAF – the war in Europe was almost over – and he trained at a local gym in West Hartlepool, did his roadwork along the sea front, and fitted in a lot of swimming as part of his training programme.

Jack Solomons was a master of publicity and there were stories in the press of how Jack London's sons were giving up their egg ration for their father; and Jack, his wife Agnes and their two sons were photographed outside the Olympia Exhibition which carried the caption 'London Triumphant' on a billboard in the background.

On the eve of the fight Jack London stayed at the Pastoria Hotel in Leicester Square and Bruce Woodwork at a modest hotel in Dalston. Jack ate a hearty breakfast of poached eggs on toast and at the weigh-in on the afternoon of 17 July 1945 London tipped the scales at 15st. 5lbs to Woodcock's 13st. Both boxers then retired to their hotels for the customary rest before the fight. London was favourite to win with the bookmakers at 5-1 on.

According to Jack Solomons, 26,479 people paid to see the London-Woodcock fight, not the 40,000 sometimes reported in books and articles, and among the spectators were two trainloads of

Woodcock supporters from Doncaster. Nevertheless, it was still a good gate and the weather was kind to Jack Solomons, an important factor in an open-air promotion. Jack London was caught up in traffic congestion on his way to White Hart Lane in the evening and he was late in arriving at the ground. An anxious Jack Solomons went out to look for him and he had the greatest difficulty in getting back in. He had no ticket or pass and the door-keepers refused to believe that he was Jack Solomons. When he eventually managed to regain entry he was relieved to find that Jack London had turned up. Both champion and challenger were in their dressing rooms and ready for action when their fight was called, and as Jack London climbed through the ropes he could feel reasonably confident that he would beat off Woodcock's challenge. He was fit, two stones heavier than Woodcock, and vastly more experienced. Woodcock was, at this stage of his boxing career, an excellent heavyweight prospect : he was fast, with a good straight left and he carried a knockout punch in his right hand.

The first four rounds went badly for London : the timing of his punches was poor. Woodcock moved faster and scored freely with his left jab. In the fifth round, London switched to Woodcock's body and he made the Yorkshireman grunt as he thumped him in the ribs, and then caught Woodcock with good punches on the nose and mouth. This was London's best round. In round six London resumed his attack on Woodcock's body and in doing so dropped his guard. Woodcock's right hand flashed out at London's exposed jaw and the champion was sent sprawling against the bottom rope. London got up at the count of two, looking shaken. Woodcock took his chance and banged two more crisp rights to London's chin. Jack went down again and was struggling to get to his feet when he was counted out.

London said after the fight that he had not heard the count because of the noise of the crowd and had misjudged the time he was down on the canvas: he had intended taking a count of nine before continuing the fight. Be that as it may, there was no doubt that Bruce Woodcock was the new champion. London had held the British and Empire titles for ten months.

6

AN OLD WARHORSE

Jack London did not have a romantic view of boxing. To him it was his trade and he practised it to the best of his ability. He did not enjoy the grind of training and he approached each fight coolly and dispassionately. Some of London's critics said that the lack of a bit of devil in his makeup was one of his weaknesses as a fighter. For better or for worse, Jack London had a workmanlike approach to boxing and an equable temper to match. After he had lost his titles he was regarded as something of an old warhorse : a former champ who could be matched against younger boxers to test their mettle. Of course he was immensely proud of having won the British and Empire titles, and regretted that he had not been given his title chance in 1938 or 1939 when he was in his prime, and he was disappointed that he was never allowed the opportunity of meeting Tommy Farr or Len Harvey in the ring. However he did not feel bitter about these things, that was not his nature, and he looked ahead to his next fight. Therefore it came as no surprise to those who knew him when a fortnight after losing his titles he stepped into the ring again. On 1 August 1945 he travelled to Paisley where he was outpointed over 10 rounds by the leading contender for the Scottish heavyweight title, Jock Porter.

After the fight London admitted that it had been a mistake to agree to meet Porter so soon after his title bout, when his ribs were still sore after the Woodcock fight. However the arrangements for the Porter contest had been made several weeks before and he had not wanted to let down the promoters who had organised the charity bill in aid of the Newspaper Press Fund. Jack London added that he had decided to retire from the ring. There was not much space for sports coverage in the economy-sized newspapers of the time but sports writers found room to acknowledge Jack London's contribution to boxing over many years and they agreed that his decision to retire was the right one.

Jack London was demobilised from the RAF in October 1945 and returned to his home town where he opened a gymnasium and invested in a garage. He kept whippets as a hobby and enjoyed having a few bets at local dog-tracks. Unfortunately his business ventures were not very successful and after a few months he decided to return to the ring. He got back into training and found that his services were not in great demand in Britain, although he received several offers to fight abroad. He travelled to Stockholm, where on 2 June 1946 he was outpointed by Olle Tandberg, a clever Swedish boxer, who later defeated the formidable Joe Baksi.

Then came an offer to fight in South Africa and Jack went to earn some money and soak up a bit of sunshine. London was matched against the South African heavyweight champion Nick Wolmaraus, and the fight was arranged to take place in Johannesburg on 24 August 1946. Johannesburg lies 6,000 feet above sea level and Jack London flew out three weeks before the fight date to get used to the high altitude. The fight had been arranged to test Wolmaraus with some outside opposition. London was, of course, a former Empire titleholder, and was still remembered by many South African boxing fans as the man who had given their countryman, Ben Foord, a couple of hard fights in the 1930s.

Wolmaraus proved to be a game opponent but no match for the more ringwise Jack London, who outpointed him over 10 rounds. A couple of weeks later London knocked out Joe Foord in the sixth round at Durban, and stayed on for another three weeks to enjoy a holiday and do some sightseeing. He thoroughly enjoyed his stay in South Africa. London liked the country, then enjoying an economic boom under Prime Minister Jan Smuts who believed in maintaining close links with Britain, and he was made to feel very welcome. It was just the filip he needed and his victories over two leading South African fighters proved that he was still a force to be reckoned with in the boxing world.

It was now over a year since Bruce Woodcock had won the heavyweight championship, and he was coming under pressure to defend his titles. The West Hartlepool promoter, Walter Hazeltine, offered Woodcock a purse of £1,000 to meet Jack London in a rematch for the title, and Fred Charlton, more realistically, was prepared to go up to £3,000 in order to stage the fight at New St James's Hall. Woodcock's manager, Tom Hurst was not interested in these offers: he had his own plans for Bruce Woodcock and Jack London did not figure in them.

On 4 December 1946 the editor of *Boxing News* penned a front page article 'The Challenge of Jack London' arguing that Jack London was the logical contender for the British title and that he would provide Bruce Woodcock with the kind of opposition the Yorkshireman needed. Jack London at the age of 33 was back in the picture and the new year opened with a £500 side-stake challenge to Jack from Alf Brown the Catford heavyweight. Brown was a former British Army heavyweight champion who was ambitious to meet Bruce Woodcock for the British title and saw a victory over Jack London as advancing his prospects. The London-Brown match did not take place, but both men appeared on the same bill against different opponents at the Seymour Hall, London, on 18 February 1947 when Jack London knocked out the Dutch heavyweight champion, Jan Klein, in the first round; and Alf Brown knocked out Reg Andrews in the eighth round to become Southern Area heavyweight champion. Brown was just below London in the British heavyweight ratings and he fancied his chances against the West Hartlepool fighter, but when they were eventually matched to fight at Newcastle upon Tyne later in the year London had to pull out with an injured hand. The two men never did meet in the ring.

Another fighter keen to meet Jack London in 1947 was the giant Jamaican heavyweight, Charlie Brown , who was billed as the 'West Indian Canera". A Jack London-Charlie Brown contest would have

SEYMOUR HALL
Manager: EUGENE FIELDS

BOXING TOURNAMENT
TUESDAY, FEB. 18, 7 p.m.

Promoter   MARK SALMON
Matchmaker   BENNY HUNTMAN

International Heavyweight Contest

JACK LONDON (West Hartlepool) former Heavyweight Champion of England, V.

JAN KLEIN Official Heavyweight Champion of Holland

Southern Area Heavyweight Championship

ALF BROWN (Catford) k.o. Jock Porter (one rd.); Charlie Collett (one rd.); Al Delaney, etc., etc. Heavyweight Champion of the British Army. V.

REG ANDREWS (Streatham) Undefeated as a Heavyweight.

DICKIE O'SULLIVAN	v.	**JIMMY GILL**
JACKIE RANKIN	v.	**GUS FORAN**
RANDOLPH TURPIN	v.	**JOHNNY BEST**
JIMMY SHOORD	v.	**BILLY STILLWELL**

Tickets: £5.5.0 (Ringside), £3.3.0, £2.2.0, £1.10.0, £1.1.8, 10/6 (Standing).

Obtainable from: Joe Goodwin, Joe Wilson and Seymour Hall Box Office.

Poster, 18 February 1947.

made a good match but it was never made, instead Charlie Brown met Alf Brown and they fought a draw.

London followed his win over Klein with a second round knockout victory over the South African, Jimmy Britt, who had been one of Joe Baksi's sparring partners. The London-Britt fight took place before a 5,000 capacity crowd at the Engineers' Club Grounds in West Hartlepool. Thousands of disappointed boxing fans were locked out of the stadium and 150 policemen had to be rushed to the ground to control the people milling about outside. A fortnight later at Walthamstow, London stopped Fernand Honore in the third round. Jack London had fought his way back into contention and his reward was a place in the eliminators for the British title.

The Board of Control ruled that Jack London should meet Ken Shaw, the Scottish heavyweight champion, and the winner of this bout would face Freddie Mills for the right to meet Bruce Woodcock for the British and Empire titles. London had already beaten Shaw and Mills, if he did so again a title match would be his. The glory road was open to him.

Unfortunately, London failed at the first hurdle. He turned in a lacklustre performance against Shaw who won on points over 12 rounds, although London's poor showing should not detract from Shaw's victory. Scotland has produced many top-class fighters in the lighter divisions but very few heavies. Veteran sports journalist, Malcolm Turner of the *Scottish Daily Express* , rated Ken Shaw the best Scottish heavyweight he had seen. The Dundee fighter had an impressive record as an amateur before turning professional in 1942 and he had spent three months fighting in American rings as a preparation for the London fight. When Shaw met Freddie Mills in the final eliminator he was stopped in the first round with a badly cut lip, and Mills went on to be knocked out in the fourteenth round when he met Bruce Woodcock in the championship fight.

Jack London could not complain that he has not been given his chance and there was nothing for him but to fight on. He ended the year with points victories over Al Robinson and the Belgian heavyweight, Piet Wilde.

London was now 34 years old and around the same age as Joe

Louis, Jersey Joe Walcott, Archie Moore and Gus Lesnevitch who were still at the top. Jack London did not feel ready to retire from the ring and he was still rated number two, after Ken Shaw, among Britain's heavyweight fighters. However, as things turned out, he had no fights in 1948. Perhaps the most important events for Jack London in 1948 were that he moved house from West Hartlepool to Blackpool and changed his manager: in September, after lengthy negotiations, he signed up with George Dingley.

In March 1948 he was being lined up to meet the Austrian heavyweight, Jo Weiden, but the fight had to be called off after Jack London had received minor injuries in a car crash. In the following month, with London fully recovered from his mishap, a Lancashire promoter was interested in matching Jack London with Bruce Woodcock in a non-title fight. This match would have been a warm-up bout for Woodcock, following his long lay-off after the battering he had taken at the hands of Joe Baksi, and would have tested Woodcock's fitness before he defended his titles against challenger, Freddie Mills. A Woodcock-London rematch staged in the North of England would have drawn the crowds, but Woodcock's manager, Tom Hurst, preferred to retain his close links with Jack Solomons and the American heavyweight, Lee Oma, was drafted in by Solomons to provide Woodcock with his first comeback bout. The fight turned out to be a stinker. Oma put up a poor show and everyone was left wondering if Woodcock had fully recovered from his injuries. Bruce Woodcock won his next fight against another American, Lee Savold, on a fourth round disqualification without resolving the question of whether he had recovered his former fitness and form. When London's new manager, George Dingley, surveyed the British heavyweight scene in 1948 he was confident that Jack would have another chance of fighting for a title.

An attempt was made in 1948 to tempt Jack London into taking up wrestling. After all, ex-boxers Primo Canera and Tony Galento were pursuing highly successful wrestling careers in the USA. The tempter was Jack Pye billed as 'the first gentleman of the mat' and one of the top box-office draws in British wrestling. Jack Pye, originally from Doncaster, owned a night-club in Blackpool where he met Jack London and tried to persuade him to take up the grappling game. London, however, had painful memories of a mixed boxing-wrestling bout he had fought in the RAF. His opponent was the Scottish heavyweight wrestler, Tony Baer, who was also serving in the RAF. The contest ended when the pair crashed awkwardly to the boards, London dislocating his shoulder and Baer injuring his back. 'Never again', said London and he firmly resisted Jack Pye's offer to introduce him to the grunt and groan game.

Jack London made a good start to 1949. At Middlesbrough on 7 February 1949 he met the fighting marine from Deal, Reg Andrews. Andrews was rated fifth among Britain's heavyweights and London outpointed him over eight rounds. In the following month London dropped a points decision to Piet Wilde, and in May he won a rematch with Reg Andrews. London stopped the Belgian heavyweight, Prosper Beck, in five rounds, and won a points victory over Canadian, Don Mogard.

The Boxing Board of Control then included Jack London in the elimination series to provide a challenger for Bruce Woodcock's British Empire title. London was matched with the Canadian Vern Escoe. The winner of this contest would meet Johnny Williams from Rugby, and the winner of this bout would be matched with former guardsman, Jack Gardner. The winner to emerge from this process would have the right to meet Bruce Woodcock for the Empire title. London was being given the opportunity of meeting Britain's rising, young heavyweights – Williams and Gardner – but first he had to dispose of Vern Escoe.

Vern Escoe was a black fighter from Toronto who held the Canadian heavyweight title. He had fought professionally since 1943, including experience in American rings. He had come to Britain earlier in the year attracted by the boxing boom, and in his first fight in this country had stopped Jack Gardner in the fifth round.

The London-Escoe bout took place at the West Hartlepool Greyhound Stadium on 29 August 1949 and the crowds rolled up to watch big Jack in action. Escoe was loudly urged by his cornermen to 'Hustle the old guy', but London was capable of doing a bit of hustling on his own account and he was on top by the sixth round when he threw a right hand punch that tore a muscle in his shoulder. He was forced to retire and looked dejected as he left the ring to receive medical attention for his injured shoulder while the referee raised Escoe's arm in victory.

Three months later Jack London entered the ring against Aaron Wilson at Earls Court. Wilson was a black fighter from Knoxville, Tennessee. A former US marine he had spent a couple of years campaigning in European rings. The fight was over very quickly. In the opening exchanges Wilson caught London's right ear with a left hand wallop. London went down dazed and unbalanced by the blow, and failed to clear the canvas in time to beat the count. It was only the fifth time he had been counted out in a boxing career stretching over 18 years. Jack London decided that it would be the last: after the fight he announced his retirement from the ring.

7

ALL MY SONS

After his retirement from boxing, London and his family settled down in a bungalow in Blackpool. Jack had been stationed in Blackpool during the war and he liked the seaside town with its crowds of holiday makers in search of a bit of fun. It was a wrench to leave West Hartlepool but Jack felt he wanted to make a fresh start.

Jack London after 141 contests spread over 18 years in the ring had none of the familiar features of many former professional boxers. He had no cauliflower ears, flattened nose or scar tissue above the eyes. His main problems as a boxer had been injuries to his hands and he had suffered some fractured ribs. Jack London retired unmarked and in good physical shape. He was always dressed smartly and invariably wore a homburg hat or trilby. He was a man with natural dignity and was widely respected. The fact that he had been British and Empire heavyweight champion and worn the Lonsdale Belt were honours that followed him throughout his life. He was proud of his boxing career but was also modest about his achievements in the ring. He was only 36 years old when he retired from boxing and he had no nest-egg on which he could live for the rest of his life. London had to find a job and he reconsidered Jack Pye's suggestion that he should move into the wrestling game.

Wrestling was enjoying a boom and there was demand for grapplers. Former heavyweight boxers such as Jack Doyle, Larry

Gains, Eddie Phillips and Alf Robinson were embarking on new careers as matmen and Jack London decided that he would do the same. He attended one of the local gyms frequented by wrestlers and set about learning some of the holds and moves of the game. After a few weeks of training he was ready to face his first opponent on the mat. The bout went well and London spent the next two years appearing on wrestling bills across the country, although he never became a top-of-the-bill performer. When he faced 'mat villains' he was usually bounced around the ring in the early rounds and given a rough time, he then fought back with a series of forearm smashes. His wrestling career ended when he broke his ribs in a bad fall, aggravating a fracture he had suffered when in training for his heavyweight title fight with Freddie Mills. He was laid up for three months and suffered considerable pain from the injury.

After recovery he looked for alternative work and found a job as the manager of a night-club in Manchester. Jack was still a well known figure in North West England and therefore a good front-man for the club and he could handle any rough-stuff from unruly customers.

However he was soon to be caught up in boxing once again. His sons, John and Brian, had been schoolboy boxers and had grown up into strapping youths. Both were drawn to boxing and Jack London became absorbed in promoting their careers. Although John was keener on the sport than his younger brother, it was Brian who enjoyed greater success in the ring.

John was called up to do his national service in the RAF in 1951 and became a physical training instructor. He took part in service boxing and became light heavyweight champion of the RAF and a member of the RAF boxing team. After completing his national service in 1954 he left the amateur ranks and boxed professionally until 1966, mainly in eight round bouts. In 1952 Brian followed his brother into the RAF and he too became a physical training instructor like his father and brother before him. He did his trade training at RAF Cosford and passed out from his course as a corporal. He was then posted to RAF Weeton. During his off-duty hours he did some cross country running and enjoyed a game of football. However when his commanding officer discovered that Corporal Brian Harper of the sports section was the son of Jack London he drafted him into the station boxing team and Corporal Harper went on to become the heavyweight champion of the RAF. In 1954 he won the Empire Games and the ABA heavyweight titles, and when he was demobilised from the RAF later in the year he turned professional, adopting the ring name Brian London. His brother fought as Jack London Jr. and they often appeared on the same bill. Jack London helped to train them and was always at the ringside when they boxed. The London boys fought several of their first professional bouts at West Hartlepool and were accompanied by their father who received a warm welcome from the crowd on his return to his home town.

Brian won 20 of his first 23 fights and on 3 June 1958 he was matched with Joe Erskine for the British and Empire heavyweight titles. The press knew a good angle when they saw one, and Jack London was heavily featured training with the son who was going after his former titles. The Blackpool Bomber knocked out Erskine in the eighth round to become the new champion, setting up a new record as the first father and son to win the same titles. Brian London beat the highly-rated American, Willie Pastrano, in his next fight but lost the British and Empire titles to Henry Cooper on 12 January 1959. In spite of this defeat he was matched with Floyd Paterson for the world heavyweight title, against the wishes of the British Boxing Board of Control. The fight took place at Indianapolis with brother Jack appearing on the same bill. The whole London family travelled to the USA for the fight and Jack was at the ringside as usual when his boys were in action in the ring. He was immensely proud of his sons' boxing achievements, although Paterson stopped Brian in the eleventh round to retain the world title. Jack London was also pleased to see his sons getting financial returns from the boxing game far in excess of anything he had earned.

In the following year Jack London found himself in the limelight again although this time in less favourable circumstances. At the Coney Beach Arena, Porthcawl, on 29 August 1960 Brian faced

Engineers' Club Grounds
WEST HARTLEPOOL

BOXING

Licensed under British Boxing Board of Control.   Promoter : W. Hazeltine

Admission - 2/3 4/- and 6/- (inc. Tax)
PROGRAMME - PRICE 3d.

Brian London   **Jack London (father)**   **Jack London**

(Photographs by courtesy of the "NORTHERN DAILY MAIL")

RACING, FOOTBALL
GREYHOUNDS

JOHN JOYCE
COMMISSION AGENT

Established 20 years.   Bankers : Martins Bank Ltd.
Telephone 4191 (5 lines).   Private 3782
Write or Phone for Credit Account.

202 York Road, West Hartlepool

I personally attend all North Country Meetings—Tattersalls Ring

*Programme 23 May 1955 : Brian London v Hugh McDonald and
Jack London Jr. v Ken Wyatt.*

Dick Richardson for the European heavyweight title, and Jack London was at the ringside. It was a bad tempered contest and there was much vocal support from both corners. Brian London boxed well for the first seven rounds and was clearly ahead on points when he sustained a cut eye in round eight. On making his way back to his corner at the end of the round Brian London turned to Richardson's corner and said: 'Watch his head, ref.' Tempers were already stretched to breaking point and the ringside erupted. Insults were flung by both sides and Richardson's cornermen leapt into the ring and were met by Brian London's handlers led by Jack London. The former champion, noted for his equable temper during his years in the ring, was livid with rage as he exchanged punches with Richardson's supporters in the centre of the canvas square. The arena was in uproar for several minutes until boxing officials and ushers managed to restore order and Brian London announced his retirement from the contest. This brouhaha, together with Jack London's role in it, was given wide coverage in the media and the Boxing Board of Control carried out an inquiry into what had caused the disturbance. The incident did not upset Brian London's boxing career. He carried on boxing and his father continued to give him his support.

Jack's wife, Agnes, died in 1962. She had been a loyal wife to her husband over the years and in spite of the fact that Jack had enjoyed a couple of well-publicised affairs with younger women she had been prepared to welcome him back into the family fold. Jack appeared to have got over his bereavement and to be in good health when it was reported that he had died in his sleep at his flat in Pittsdale Avenue, Blackpool, on 19 December 1963. A post-mortem revealed that he had suffered a heart attack and an inquest was not considered necessary. He was 50 years old. A service followed by cremation took place at the Carleton Crematorium, Blackpool, on Monday 23 December 1963. The service was attended by the family, friends and members of the boxing fraternity, including Peter Kane, the former world flyweight champion, a close friend who had served with Jack in the RAF.

In reporting his death the press linked Jack with the hard days of the 1930s, when there were long dole queues and boxers fought for small purses and were grateful for the chance of a spot on a boxing bill. As a former British and Empire champion Jack London rated an obituary in *The Times* and it summed up his career with the words:

If not by any means one of the great champions and certainly not one of the most skilful, he was nevertheless a big, strong man who could be a formidable performer on his day.

JACK LONDON'S BOXING RECORD
1931–1949

1931

Jul 10	Barney Stockton	W ko 1	Hartlepool *
Jul 18	Battling Manners	W dis 1	Hartlepool
Jul 20	Phil Henry	W ko 5	Stockton
Jul 31	Jack Wharton	W pts 10	Middlesbrough
Aug 22	Jim Williams	W pts 10	Newcastle upon Tyne
Aug 30	Eddie Strawer	L pts 12	Royton
Sep 12	Corporal Ingledew	W ko 7	Hartlepool
Sep 20	Tommy Moore	L pts 12	Barnsley
Sep 28	Jack Smith	L pts 10	Hartlepool
Oct 16	Tom Powell	L pts 10	Hartlepool
Oct 21	Willie Duncan	L pts 10	Edinburgh
Oct 24	Jim Williams	W ko 2	Newcastle upon Tyne
Oct 26	Frank Bagley	L pts 10	Newcastle upon Tyne
Oct 30	Tom Powell	W ko 6	Stockton
Dec 14	Chris Rock	L pts 12	Durham
Dec 25	Jack Smith	L pts 10	Backworth

1932

Jan 16	Frank Bagley	Drew 10	Hartlepool
Jan 18	Joe Morrison	W rtd 5	Newcastle upon Tyne
Feb 6	Jack Clansey	L pts 10	Hartlepool
Mar 18	Dick Bartlett	W pts 10	Hartlepool
Mar 26	Frank Bagley	Drew 10	Hartlepool
Apr 8	Gunner Ainsley	W rsf 9	Hartlepool
Apr 22	Corporal Dorry	W ko 1	Hartlepool
May 6	Dick Bartlett	W ko 5	Hartlepool
May 11	Tom Powell	W ret 3	Stockton
May 13	Paul McGuire	W pts 10	Hartlepool
Jun 24	Charlie McDonald	L pts 12	Hartlepool
Sep 10	Bill Brennan	W ko 3	Hartlepool
Sep 23	Guardsman Gater	W pts 12	Hartlepool
Oct 23	Jack O'Malley	L rtd 7	Blackfriars
Dec 2	Jack Strongbow	W rtd 10	Hartlepool

1933

Jan 6	Dick Bartlett	W rtd 6	Hartlepool
Jan 16	Charlie McDonald	W pts 12	Newcastle upon Tyne
Jan 27	Eddie Strawer	W pts 12	Hartlepool
Feb 10	Bert Ikin	W pts 10	Hartlepool
Feb 27	Jack Morris	W rtd 6	Newcastle upon Tyne
Mar 24	Les Saunders	NC 3	Hartlepool
Apr 8	Battling Sullivan	W rtd 5	Hartlepool
Apr 10	Gipsy Daniels	L rtd 6	Merthyr
Apr 30	Al Conquest	W pts 12	Leeds
May 18	Bobby Shields	W ko 2	Norton on Tees
May 20	Al Arpino	W pts 15	Merthyr

May 26	George Slack	Drew 12	Hartlepool
Jun 5	Battling Sullivan	W rsf 7	Newcastle upon Tyne
Jun 12	Jack Casey	L rtd 10	Hartlepool
Jul 3	Con van Lewen	W rtd 8	Hartlepool
Jul 17	Gipsy Daniels	L pts 12	Hartlepool
Jul 31	Gipsy Daniels	Drew 12	Hartlepool
Aug 31	Len Johnson	L pts 12	Liverpool
Sep 25	Johnny Rice	W dis 6	Hartlepool
Nov 6	Ben Foord	L pts 10	Crystal Palace
Dec 4	Seaman Harry Rowles	W pts 12	Crystal Palace
Dec 11	Larry Gains	L ko 2	Newcastle upon Tyne

1934

Jan 15	Charlie Smith	L pts 12	Crystal Palace
Jan 21	George Slack	L pts 12	Middlesbrough
Feb 5	Frank Borrington	W pts 10	Crystal Palace
Feb 16	George Slack	L pts 12	Bradford
Apr 29	Bert Melzow	L dis 11	Rotherham
May 21	Jack Pettifer	Drew 10	Brighton
Jun 4	Charlie Belanger	L dis 8	Newcastle upon Tyne
Jul 16	Jack Strongbow	W pts 12	Hartlepool
Jul 28	Pierre Charles	L ko 1	Ostend
Oct 8	Charlie Belanger	L ko 3	Hull
Oct 14	Johnny Rice	W rsf 9	Blackfriars
Nov 5	Alex Bell	W pts 10	Crystal Palace
Nov 18	Alex Bell	W pts 10	Blackfriars
Dec 3	Italo Colonello	W pts 10	Crystal Palace

1935

Jan 3	Frank Borrington	W pts 12	West Ham
Jan 28	Jack Pettifer	W ko 4	Crystal Palace
Feb 7	Alex Bell	L dis 9	Edinburgh
Feb 25	Ben Foord	L pts 12	Plymouth
Mar 7	George Slack	W rtd 10	West Ham
May 25	Jack Casey	W pts 12	Sunderland
Jun 17	Helmuth Hartkopp	W ko 2	Newcastle upon Tyne
Jul 29	Charlie Smith	W rtd 2	Newcastle upon Tyne
Oct 8	Jack Strongbow	W ko 2	Wembley
Nov 12	Ginger Hauxwell	W rsf 4	Wembley
Nov 12	Johnny Rice	W ko 3	Wembley
Nov 23	Ginger Hauxwell	W ko 3	Middlesbrough
Dec 9	Eddie Steele	W pts 12	Hartlepool

1936

Jan 29	Eddie Houghton	W pts 6	Wembley
Feb 1	Roy Lazer	W pts 12	Brighton
Mar 2	Frank Borrington	W ko 9	Derby
Mar 11	Maurice Strickland	W pts 10	Belfast
Mar 16	Tommy Loughran	L pts 10	Bristol
Jun 15	Obie Walker	W pts 10	Leicester
Oct 7	Hans Schonrath	W pts 10	Berlin
Oct 19	Larry Gains	NC 8	Earls Court
Nov 9	Pat Marrinan	W dis 6	Wembley

1937

Jan 25	Bob Carvill	W pts 15	Hartlepool

(Eliminator for Northern Area heavyweight title)

Feb 3	Harry Staal	L pts 10	York
Mar 8	Pancho Villar	W ko 2	Bristol
Mar 15	George Bennett	W ko 2	Newcastle upon Tyne

(Final eliminator for Northern Area heavyweight title)

May 24	Buddy Baer	L pts 10	Swansea
Jul 19	Jim Wilde	W ko 3	Swansea
Nov 29	Manuel Abrew	W ko 6	Harringay

1938

Feb 7	Hans Schonrath	W pts 10	Bristol
Apr 11	Harry Staal	W pts 10	Bristol
Jun 27	Al Delaney	L dis 4	New Cross
Jul 15	Harry Lister	W dis 10	Easington
Aug 4	Joe Zeman	W ko 3	Hartlepool
Aug 22	Charlie Bundy	W ko 3	Hartlepool
Sept 2	Al Delaney	W pts 10	Manchester
Dec 12	Alf Luxton	W rsf 1	Hartlepool
Dec 18	George Cook	W ko 2	Blackfriars

1939

Mar 2	Al Delaney	W ko 8	Albert Hall
Apr 3	George James	W pts 12	Mountain Ash
Aug 10	Jean Verbeeran	W ko 1	Hartlepool
Nov 27	Tommy Martin	L pts 10	Earls Court
Dec 9	Tom Reddington	W rsf 7	Harringay

1940
Apr 24	Al Robinson	W rtd 3	Newcastle upon Tyne

1941
Jan 25	Larry Gains	W ko 4	Liverpool
Feb 20	Tom Reddington	W pts 6	Odeon Theatre,
May 28	Larry Gains	W ko 3	Newcastle upon Tyne
Aug 1	Tommy Martin .	W pts 10	Manchester

(Eliminator for British Empire heavyweight title)

Dec 8	Freddie Mills	L pts 10	Albert Hall

1942
Jun 6	Larry Gains	W ko 2	Dundee
Aug 16	Jim Wilde	W rtd 3	Wrexham

1943
Mar 8	Jim Wilde	W rtd 2	Wolverhampton
Mar 29	Al Robinson	W ko 8	Leicester

1944
Mar 17	George James	W pts 6	Thorney Island
Sept 5	Freddie Mills	W pts 15	Manchester

(British and British Empire heavyweight titles)

1945

Jun 15	Ken Shaw	W rtd 8	Hartlepool
Jul 17	Bruce Woodcock	L ko 6	Tottenham

(British and British Empire heavyweight titles)

Aug 1	Jock Porter	L pts 10	Paisley

1946

Jun 2	Olle Tandberg	L pts 10	Stockholm
Aug 24	Nick Walmaraus	W pts 10	Johannesburg
Sept 4	Joe Foord	W ko 6	Durban

1947

Feb 18	Jan Klein	W ko 1	Marylebone
May 5	James Britt	W ko 2	Hartlepool
May 19	Fernand Honore	W rsf 3	Walthamstow
Jun 9	Ken Shaw	L pts 12	Manchester

(Eliminator for British and British Empire heavyweight titles)

Sept 9	Al Robinson	W pts 8	Leeds
Oct 6	Piet Wilde	W pts 10	Nottingham

1949

Feb 7	Reg Andrews	W pts 8	Middlesbrough
Mar 21	Piet Wilde	L pts 8	Middlesbrough
May 2	Reg Andrews	W pts 8	Hartlepool
Jun 13	Prosper Beck	W rsf 5	Hartlepool
Jul 25	Don Mogard	W pts 8	Hartlepool
Aug 29	Vern Escoe	L rtd 6	Hartlepool

(Eliminator for British Empire heavyweight title)

Nov 29	Aaron Wilson	L ko 1	Earls Court

Contests	141
Won	95
Drew	5
Lost	39
No Contest	2

Key:

W	(won)
L	(lost)
NC	(no contest)
pts	(points)
ko	(knockout)
rtd	(retired)
rsf	(referee stopped fight)
dis	(disqualified)

*The towns of Hartlepool and West Hartlepool were merged into a single borough to be known as Hartlepool on 1 April 1967, and I have used this name to cover both of the former towns.

BIBLIOGRAPHY

The magazines *Boxing, Boxing News* and *The Ring* are the main sources for fight reports and other developments in the boxing world. There are several local newspapers that have been essential sources of information, namely *Hartlepool Mail, Newcastle Evening Chronicle, Newcastle Journal, Northern Daily Mail, Northern Echo, Sunday Sun* and *Sunderland Echo.* Articles deserving special mention are: 'Jack London's Own Story' – five autobiographical articles that appeared in the Northern edition of the *Daily Express* 2-6 August 1960; Blue Bird's Eye, 'Cinderella Man Jack London', *Boxing News* 8 August 1945; Fred Charlton, 'The fighting enigma who became Empire champion', *Sunderland Echo* 18 November 1967; and Gilbert Odd, 'London's hard road to glory', *Boxing News* 20 August 1976.

Some useful autobiographies include: Tommy Farr, *Thus Farr* (London 1989); Larry Gains, *The Impossible Dream* (London no date); Freddie Mills,*Twenty Years* (London 1950) and *Battling for a Title* (London 1954); Jack Solomons, *Jack Solomons Tells All* (London 1951); Peter Wilson, *The Man They Could Not Gag* (London 1977); and Bruce Woodcock, *Two Fists and a Fortune* (London 1951).

Biographies include: Archie Potts, *Jack Casey the Sunderland Assassin* (Whitley Bay 1991); Michael Taub, *Jack Doyle – Fighting for Love* (London 1990); Bob Lonkhurst, *Man of Courage: the life and career of Tommy Farr* (Lewes 1997); Gilbert Odd, *Len Harvey – Prince of Boxers* (London 1978); Michael Herbert, *Never Counted Out -the story of Len Johnson* (Manchester 1992); Jack Birley, *Freddie Mills -his life and death* (London 1977), Tony Van Den Bergh, *Who Killed Freddie Mills?* (London 1991) and Peter McInnes, *Freddie My Friend* (Chippenham 1995).

Books providing local background include: Brian Donald, *The Fight Game in Scotland* (Edinburgh 1988); F.C. Moffat, *Linament and Leather – sixty years of the fight game in the North* (Durham 1981); Archie Potts, *The Wearside Champions* (Whitley Bay 1993); Robert Smith *Hartlepool Professional Boxers – the Golden Decade 1945-55* (Hartlepool 1985); and Robert Wood, *West Hartlepool the rise and development of a Victorian new town* (West Hartlepool 1967).

For general background there are: Frank Butler, *A History of Boxing in Britain* (London 1972); John Harvey, *Lonsdale's Belt* (London 1994); and Gilbert Odd, *The Encyclopedia of Boxing* (London 1989).

Finally, two commentaries on the fight game are: Peter Wilson, *Ringside Seat* (London 1949) and *More Ringside Seats* (London 1959).